This workbook belongs to:

_____

- - - - - - - - - - - - - - -

_____

The Sound of Mm

Moose is **m**unching **m**uffins.
What else begins with the sound of **Mm**?

 each picture whose name begins
with the sound of **Mm**.

Draw a picture of something else that
begins with the sound of Mm here.

✔ *recognize the sound of initial consonant* Mm
✔ *use auditory discrimination to identify words that begin*
with the sound of Mm
✔ *associate the letter* Mm *with the sound of* Mm

Kids Can Learn with Franklin – *First Phonics*

The Sound of Ss

Soup and salad make a **s**uper **s**upper!
What else begins with the sound of **Ss**?

 each picture whose name begins
with the sound of Ss.

S s

Draw a picture of something else that
begins with the sound of Ss here.

Kids Can Learn with Franklin – *First Phonics*

The Sound of Rr

Rabbit and **R**accoon **r**eally like to **r**un.
What else begins with the sound of **Rr**?

 each picture whose name begins
with the sound of Rr.

Rr

Draw a picture of something else that
begins with the sound of Rr here.

✔ *recognize the sound of initial consonant* Rr
✔ *use auditory discrimination to identify words that begin*
  with the sound of Rr
✔ *associate the letter* Rr *with the sound of* Rr

™ Kids Can Press
© Contextx Inc. & Brenda Clark Illustrator Inc.
All rights reserved.

Kids Can Learn with Franklin – *First Phonics*

The Sound of Tt

Time to put the toys in the tub!
What else begins with the sound of Tt?

 each picture whose name begins
with the sound of Tt.

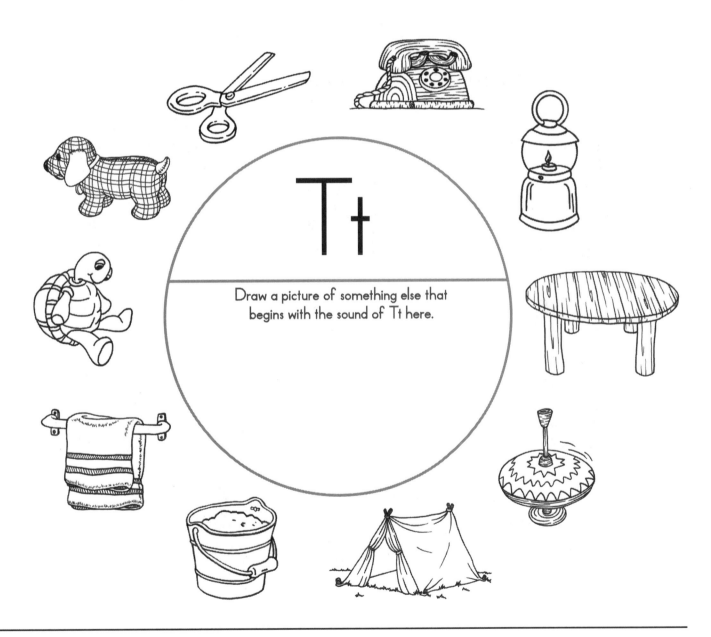

T t

Draw a picture of something else that
begins with the sound of Tt here.

Sound Review
Mm, Ss, Rr and Tt

 the letter that stands for the sound you
hear at the beginning of each picture name.

M R	S M	T R	T S
R S	M T	S M	R T

What begins with these sounds? a picture for each letter.

M	S	R	T

✔ use auditory discrimination to differentiate between the sounds of initial consonants Mm, Ss, Rr and Tt
✔ identify the written symbols for the sounds of Mm, Ss, Rr and Tt

6

Kids Can Learn with Franklin – First Phonics

The Sound of Bb

Bear has **b**erries in his **b**ike **b**asket.
What else begins with the sound of **Bb**?

 each picture whose name begins
with the sound of Bb.

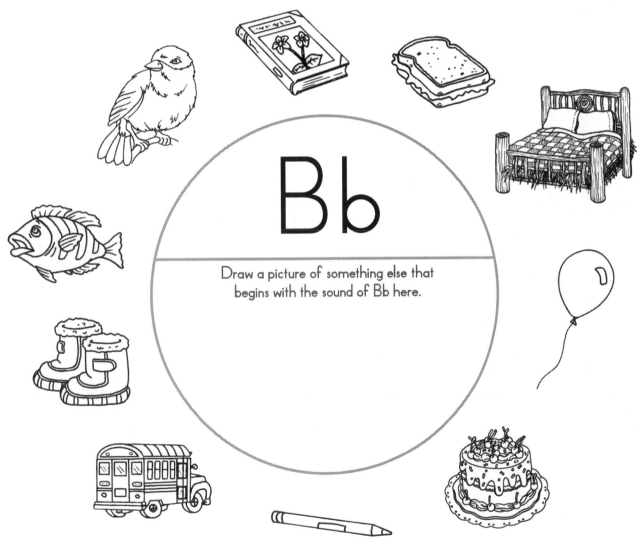

Bb

Draw a picture of something else that
begins with the sound of Bb here.

The Sound of Ff

Bear and **F**ranklin have **f**un **f**ishing.
What else begins with the sound of **Ff**?

 each picture whose name begins
with the sound of Ff.

F f

Draw a picture of something else that
begins with the sound of F f here.

✔ *recognize the sound of initial consonant* Ff
✔ *use auditory discrimination to identify words that begin*
  with the sound of Ff
✔ *associate the letter* Ff *with the sound of* Ff

The Sound of Cc

Rabbit likes to **c**runch on **c**old **c**arrots.
What else begins with the sound of **Cc**?

 each picture whose name begins
with the sound of Cc.

C c

Draw a picture of something else that
begins with the sound of Cc here.

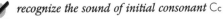 ✔ *recognize the sound of initial consonant* Cc
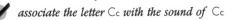 ✔ *use auditory discrimination to identify words that begin*
with the sound of Cc
✔ *associate the letter* Cc *with the sound of* Cc

™ Kids Can Press
© Contextx Inc. & Brenda Clark Illustrator Inc.
All rights reserved.

Kids Can Learn with Franklin – *First Phonics*

The Sound of Ll

Look at the lightning! Listen to the loud thunder!
What else begins with the sound of Ll?

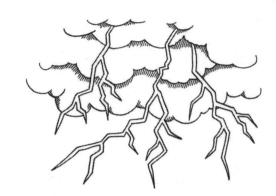

 each picture whose name begins
with the sound of Ll.

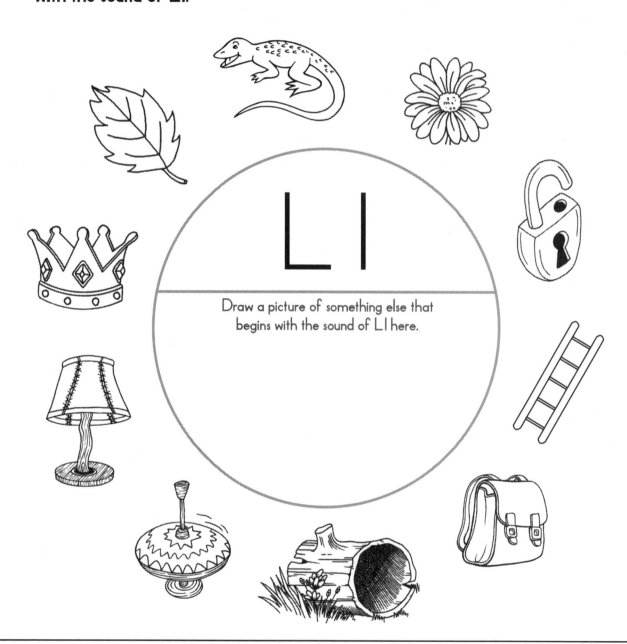

Ll

Draw a picture of something else that
begins with the sound of Ll here.

Sound Review

Bb, Ff, Cc and Ll

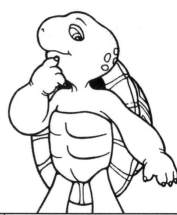

 the letter that stands for the sound you
hear at the beginning of each picture name.

B (C) F	L F	B L	C

L C	B F	L B	F C

What begins with these sounds? a picture for each letter.

B	F	C	L

✔ use auditory discrimination to differentiate between the
sounds of initial consonants Bb, Ff, Cc and Ll
✔ identify the written symbols for the sounds of
Bb, Ff, Cc and Ll

The Sound of Pp

Franklin is **p**roud of the **p**ictures he **p**ainted.
What else begins with the sound of **Pp**?

 each picture whose name begins
with the sound of Pp.

Pp

Draw a picture of something else that begins with the sound of Pp here.

Kids Can Learn with Franklin – *First Phonics*

The Sound of Hh

Franklin is **h**appy to **h**old **h**is sister, **H**arriet.
What else begins with the sound of **Hh**?

 each picture whose name begins
with the sound of Hh.

Hh

Draw a picture of something else that
begins with the sound of Hh here.

The Sound of Dd

Duck is **d**iving off the **d**ock.
What else begins with the sound of **Dd**?

 each picture whose name begins
with the sound of Dd.

Dd

Draw a picture of something else that
begins with the sound of Dd here.

 recognize the sound of initial consonant Dd

 use auditory discrimination to identify words that begin
with the sound of Dd

 associate the letter Dd with the sound of Dd

Kids Can Learn with Franklin – *First Phonics*

The Sound of Gg

Goose is a **g**reat **g**oalie!
What else begins with the sound of **Gg**?

each picture whose name begins
with the sound of **Gg**.

Gg

Draw a picture of something else that
begins with the sound of Gg here.

™ Kids Can Press
© Contextx Inc. & Brenda Clark Illustrator Inc.
All rights reserved.

Kids Can Learn with Franklin – *First Phonics*

Sound Review

Pp, Hh, Dd and Gg

 the letter that stands for the sound you
hear at the beginning of each picture name.

P D	G P	H G	D G
H D	H P	G D	H P

What begins with these sounds? a picture for each letter.

P	H	D	G

Kids Can Learn with Franklin – *First Phonics*

#22

MR. MOLE
Category: Other Faces in Woodland

Often out and about in Woodland, Mr. Mole enjoys visiting friends, including Franklin's father. Mr. Mole also likes to help with community events. One Halloween, he set up a haunted house for everyone to visit. It was pretty spooky, but lots of fun!

#40

THE POND
Category: Places in Woodland

Of the many special places in Woodland, Franklin likes the pond best of all. In winter, he and his friends play hockey. In summer, they spend their days swimming and fishing. It's the best spot for year-round fun! Of course, the pond is also where many flies and other bugs are — there are always plenty for Franklin's snack-time treat!

#90

PICNIC MICE
Category: Busy Mice

Spring has finally sprung, and the mice are having a picnic to celebrate! They're always on a mini-adventure — have you noticed them in the Franklin stories? Sometimes the mice are difficult to find, but look closely. You never know what they'll be up to next!

#10

RABBIT
Category: Franklin's Friends

Franklin's friend Rabbit is very fast, which makes him a good player to have on the soccer team! Rabbit is always up for playing sports and can even swim — with a water ring. Rabbit also likes to play leapfrog, ride his bike and play with his friends at their secret clubhouse.

Other Faces in Woodland
MR. MOLE
22

Places in Woodland
THE POND
40

Busy Mice
PICNIC MICE
90

Franklin's Friends
RABBIT
10

How many Franklin collector cards do you have?

Each workbook features 4 different cards! Build your very own set — there are lots of fun categories to collect!

Read Franklin's stories to find out more about the characters, places and things you've discovered on the collector cards in this workbook.

- Turtle Food • Franklin's Family • Homes in Woodland • Franklin's Friends • Busy Mice • Turtle Toys • Franklin's Feelings • Places in Woodland • Other Faces in Woodland • Turtle Stuff

---

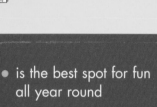

- is Franklin's father's best friend
- enjoys helping with community events

Storybook link:
Franklin's Thanksgiving

Meet Mr. Mole in
Franklin's Thanksgiving

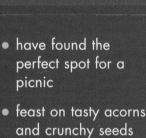

- is the best spot for fun all year round
- attracts all kinds of bugs — and a certain turtle who likes to eat them!

Storybook link:
Hurry Up, Franklin

Visit the Pond in
Hurry Up, Franklin

- have found the perfect spot for a picnic
- feast on tasty acorns and crunchy seeds

Storybook link:
Franklin and Harriet

Find the Picnic Mice in
Franklin and Harriet

- is very fast
- is always up for playing a game
- likes to play with his friends at their secret clubhouse

Storybook link:
Franklin's Secret Club

Meet Rabbit in
Franklin's Secret Club

Silly Rhyme Time

Franklin wants to bake a cake to take to the lake.
Harriet, stay awake!

What other words rhyme?

Say the names of the pictures in each box.  **a line
to connect them if they rhyme.**

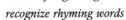
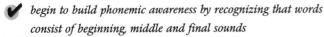

*begin to build phonemic awareness by recognizing that words
consist of beginning, middle and final sounds*

recognize rhyming words

17

Kids Can Learn with Franklin – *First Phonics*

Word Families " _at"

Listen to the sound you hear at the end of the word *cat*.
What other words end with the same sound?

 A the letter that completes each word.

b   m

b a t

h   f

_ a t

Draw a picture for your own " _at"
word here.

_ a t

Word Families " _et"

Listen to the sound you hear at the end of the word *net*.
What other words end with the same sound?

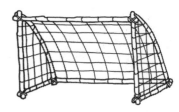

 A the letter that completes each word.

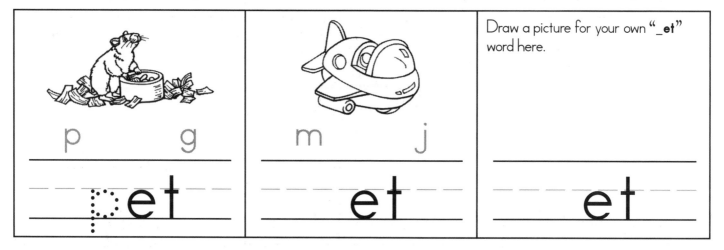

p   g

p e t

m   j

_ e t

Draw a picture for your own " _et"
word here.

_ e t

✔ *develop phonemic awareness by recognizing beginning, middle*
  and final sounds in words
✔ *identify rhyming words*
✔ *begin to apply sound–letter correspondence to decode words*

18

Kids Can Learn with Franklin – First Phonics

Word Families " _ick"

Listen to the sound you hear at the end of the word *lick*.
What other words end with the same sound?

 the letter that completes each word.

p   s

sick

k   t

ick

Draw a picture for your own " **_ick**"
word here.

ick

Word Families " _op"

Listen to the sound you hear at the end of the word *mop*.
What other words end with the same sound?

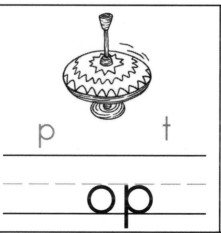

 the letter that completes each word.

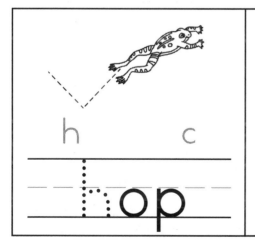

h   c

hop

p   t

op

Draw a picture for your own " **_op**"
word here.

op

✔ *develop phonemic awareness by recognizing beginning, middle*
and final sounds in words
✔ *identify rhyming words*
✔ *begin to apply sound–letter correspondence to decode words*

19

™ Kids Can Press
© Context*x* Inc. & Brenda Clark Illustrator Inc.
All rights reserved.

Kids Can Learn with Franklin – *First Phonics*

Word Families "_ug"

Listen to the sound you hear at the end of the word *hug*.
What other words end with the same sound?

 A the letter that completes each word.

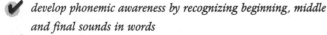		Draw a picture for your own "**_ug**" word here.
b d	m r	
b u g	_ u g	_ u g

Your Word Family

Write a word. What sound does your word end with?
What other words end with the same sound?

 **A 3 words that end in the same sound.** **a picture for each word.**

____	____	____

Kids Can Learn with Franklin – *First Phonics*

A Pad Full of Words

Franklin is glad that he found his writing pad!
He has written lots of rhyming words.
How many words can you read that sound like *pad*?

Instructions

- Glue this page onto a piece of construction paper.
- Cut out the pencil and pad of paper.
- Cut along the dotted lines to make slits in the pad.
- Slip the pencil through the slits.
- Read each new word as you slide the pencil through the pad.

Diagram

P a d

___ a d

✔ *identify rhyming words*
✔ *apply sound–letter correspondence to decode words*

Kids Can Learn with Franklin – First Phonics

This page has been left blank for the
cutout activity that appears on the previous page.

A Den Full of Words

Hurry into Fox's den! It's raining, so everyone is coming in to read. How many words can you read that sound like *den*?

Instructions

- Cut out the pages.
- The big page with the word *den* goes on the bottom.
- Put the small letter pages on top and staple everything together.
- Read each word as you flip the pages of your book.

Diagram

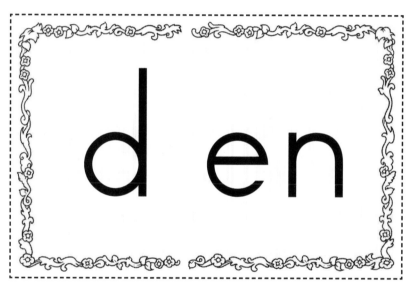

 identify rhyming words
 apply sound–letter correspondence to decode words

 23

Kids Can Learn with Franklin – *First Phonics*

This page has been left blank for the
cutout activity that appears on the previous page.

"_ock" Puzzles

Franklin likes to do puzzles. Do you?
Here are some word puzzles for you!

Instructions

- Glue this page onto a piece of construction paper.
- Cut out each word puzzle.
- Separate the puzzle pieces by cutting along the dotted line.
- Mix up all the pieces and then put the word puzzles back together again.
- Read each word.

l ock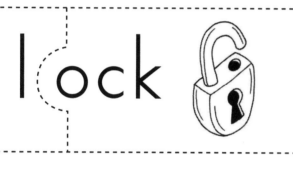

bl ock

s ock

cl ock

r ock

d ock

identify rhyming words
apply sound–letter correspondence to decode words

Kids Can Learn with Franklin – *First Phonics*

This page has been left blank for the
cutout activity that appears on the previous page.

Pig Rhymes

Franklin's big pig is full of coins!
How many words can you read that sound like *pig*?

Instructions

- Glue this page onto a piece of construction paper.
- Cut out the piggy bank and the strip of coins.
- Cut along the dotted lines to make slits in the bank.
- Slip the strip of coins into the slot.
- Read each new word as you slide the coins through the slot.

Diagram

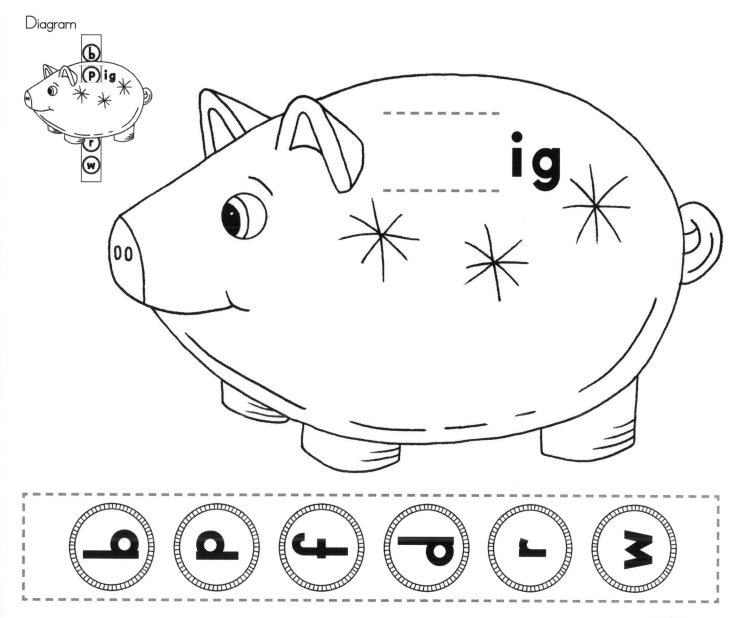

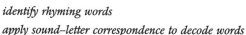

 identify rhyming words
 apply sound–letter correspondence to decode words

Kids Can Learn with Franklin – *First Phonics*

This page has been left blank for the
cutout activity that appears on the previous page.

A Sun Full of Words

Franklin loves hot days when the sun is shining bright.
How many words can you read that sound like *sun*?

Instructions

- Glue this page onto a piece of construction paper.
- Cut out the circles.
- Put the small circle on top of the big sun.
- Put a pencil or straw through the point in the middle of the sun.
- Read each new word as you turn the small circle.

Diagram

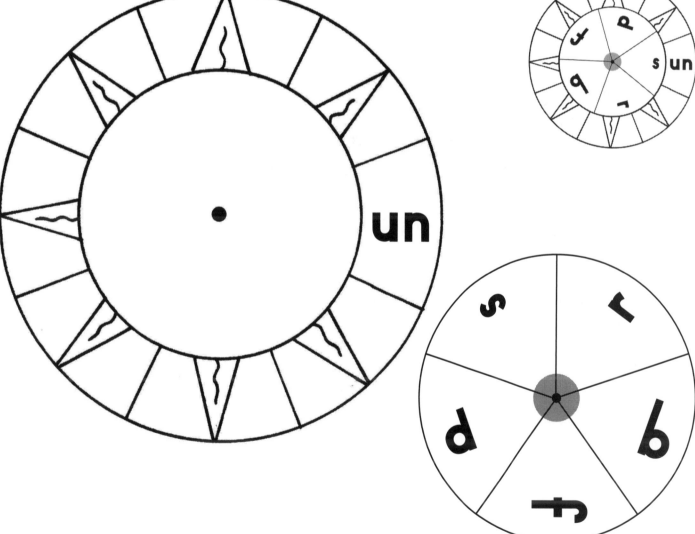

un

™ Kids Can Press
© Contextx Inc. & Brenda Clark Illustrator Inc.
All rights reserved.

Kids Can Learn with Franklin – *First Phonics*

This page has been left blank for the
cutout activity that appears on the previous page.

Franklin's Phonics Word List

balloon	bat	bed	bike	bird	book	boots	bus
cake	candles	cap	car	cat	cup	dentist	dinosaur
dishes	dog	doll	door	duck	feather	fence	fire
fish	fork	Fox	frog	game	garbage	garden	gate
ghost	goggles	hammer	hat	heart	hockey	hose	house
jet	ladder	lamp	leaf	lizard	lock	log	mask
mitts	money	moon	mouse	mushroom	net	pail	pencil
pie	pig	pillow	pumpkin	radio	rain	rake	ribbon
rug	ruler	salad	sandbox	sandwich	sled	sock	soup
sun	table	telephone	tent	top	towel	truck	turtle

_____

- - - - - - - - - - - - - - - - -

_____

name

knows lots of letters, sounds and rhyming words.

Excellent work!

_____

signature

_____

date